CHAPTER 1
What is R.E.A.L.?

R.E.A.L. stands for Responsible, Effective, Affirmed, Learning—the foundation of the GET R.E.A.L. program, which has been in existence for almost two decades. The GET R.E.A.L. program is about the mastering of strategic intervention; we can transform habitual, manipulative, self-defeating behavioral responses, and choose powerful, strategic behavioral responses.

THE GET R.E.A.L. program is based on the foundational teachings of the SLS Strategic Learning System. The SLS method is based on historical and scientific studies, as well as practical observations of the responses of the strategic, affirmative individual in invalidating situations, particularly situations of racism, sexism, and other forms of elitism.

The GET R.E.A.L. individual chooses to respond strategically, based on an objectively accurate, subjectively and acceptable self-image.

The UNR.E.A.L. individual responds in an invalidating, manipulative manner, based upon an objectively inaccurate, subjectively unacceptable self-image.

The objective is for the person to GET R.E.A.L., and face invalidating circumstances with affirmative intervention. The result is to empower the individual to become a Master of Situations.

The GET R.E.A.L. program is derived from:

1. Examining experiences of invalidation and intervention, personal and institutional.

2. Extensive research on individual and organizational behavior, particularly observations of strategic, affirmative individuals and organizations.

3. Studying, traveling, and teaching in many cultures and countries (the United States, Europe, and Canada).

4. Strategic Learning System diploma (S.L.S), Bayside, New York, A. Lee Johnson.

5. Examination of experiences, working with troubled and high-risk youth.

6. Examination of experiences, working with federal offenders for almost 30 years.

It is essential to understand and appreciate this book and be able to liberate a modern mindset. Five fundamental concepts provide the framework for transforming the self-esteem conspiracy, and liberating personal power:

1. Affirmation

2. Invalidation

3. Intervention

4. Collusion

5. Actualization

Affirmation

Acknowledgement of the beauty, sensuality, and intelligence of all human beings, without condition, qualification, reservation, or invidious comparison.

Invalidation

Insult, humiliation, patronization, paternalism, exploitation, or denial/diminishment of freedom, justice, equality, and dignity, mainly based on racist, sexist, or other elitist paradigms.

Intervention

Affirmative, strategic action, based on a well thought out plan, with concrete steps and predictable results to eliminate invalidation, collusion, and manipulation. Intervention principally takes the form of strategic behavior in four aspects: audacity, accommodation, maneuver, and discretion.

Collusion

Aiding, abetting, or accepting invalidation, avoiding intervention in situations of invalidation. Collusion principally takes the form of manipulation in four aspects: aggression, appeasement, deception, and evasion.

Actualization

The manifestation of maximum self-esteem or an objectively accurate, subjectively acceptable self-image, realized through learning strategically from every experience.

Tracking Responses

Throughout the chapter, it is vital to map out feelings and sensations, including emotions and physical responses.

Notes

Notes

CHAPTER 2
The R.E.A.L. Communication Strategy

Before moving to the next chapter, we must create R.E.A.L. communication. We must create a checklist in our mind that helps us think proactively. There are do's and don'ts to creating a strategic process.

Three Do's

1. Focus on the atmosphere.

2. Focus on feelings.

3. Focus on feedback.

Three Don'ts

1. Don't deny.

2. Don't defend.

3. Don't distort.

The GET R.E.A.L. checklist for communication is used to transform the way we think. Vigilant application of the checklist promotes the transformation of unaware to aware, nonstrategic to strategic, powerless to powerful, invalidating to affirmative.

DO'S:

1. FOCUS ON THE ENVIRONMENT

   - Listen to what is said.

   - Listen to what is not said.

   - Observe body language and context.

2. FOCUS ON FEELINGS

   - Focus on feelings.

- Focus on the feelings of others.

- Experience the feelings.

3. FOCUS ON FEEDBACK

   - Acknowledge that you are listening and observing.

   - Paraphrase what you hear and observe.

   - Give and request clarification.

DON'Ts:

1. DON'T DENY

   - Don't deny or cover up.

   - Don't deny the experience of others.

   - Don't deny feelings.

2. DON'T DEFEND

   - Don't use habitual excuses.

   - Don't use *"yeah but"* defenses.

   - Don't *become your position* in your defense of it.

3. DON'T DISTORT

   - Don't project invalidating judgments.

   - Don't project motives onto others.

   - Don't distort events and relationships.

When it comes to communication, we are highly advanced; however, we are primitive in our approach. We are very lazy when it comes to effective communication. The objective of effective communication is to send out an appropriate message, which is accurately heard and returned. It is the key to resolving most conflicts, and the cause.

For Example:

A group of co-workers attend a business luncheon. Several of the white males tell Polish *ethnic* jokes, without taking into account that the African Canadian present may perceive the jokes as a put-down.

A vice-president of a major company, being a woman, is occasionally addressed by visitors as the *secretary*.

When this person is addressed as the *secretary*, she become anxious, upset, and enraged. Potential clients are sacrificed. Another response might be more strategic.

Be aware that specific factors have particular significance. People can become unaware that other factors are equally significant.

Act without choice:

- When people are unaware that specific factors are significant.

- When people are unaware of the origin of that significance.

- When people are unaware that the significance is unexplained assumptions, and not *facts*.

- When people are unaware of the paradigmatic boundaries that have been established, and of the social interaction based on the significance.

- People may act without choice, or react on a *whim*. They may say things that they quickly regret, which limit future choices.

Choice of action is the key to strategic behavior. People may feel that their identity or beliefs (if you are aware that they are beliefs and not *facts*) are being threatened.

The individual may have difficulty seeing that it is the negative or invalidating paradigm (belief system) that is threatened by affirmation, and not the individual.

Example:

A young woman believes that she is not beautiful because she is overweight. When asked to affirm her beauty, she challenges her invalidating belief system.

The young woman becomes anxious, uncomfortable, and immobilized. She cries when asked to say, "I am beautiful."

She feels that affirmation threatens her identity, belief system, or paradigm. Her interpretation is that she is unattractive. She attaches great significance to her interpretation that she is unattractive because she is overweight.

As a result, she defines herself this way.

People may be aware; however, they also attach great significance to other culturally defined factors, such as hair. When we affirm beauty, we may attach great significance to the superiority of straight or curly hair, over kinky hair, whether you are of European or African descent.

We assume that the superiority of straight or curly hair, over kinky hair, is a fact that everyone knows and would agree upon.

We question that we might become anxious or angry. We might expose unaware, invalidating, racist beliefs about hair, which is historical and social economical in origin. We might cause embarrassment, or jeopardize a relationship.

Example:

- Specific hairstyles that can only be experienced by some.

- The man or woman who spends money and time on trying to find potions, treatments, and cures for balding.

Feeling paradigmatic anxiety is the indication that we have reached the limits or boundaries of the paradigm, identity, or belief system.

R.E.A.L. INPUT

Listen and observe.

We must ask questions for clarity.
Concentrate on what we are hearing and
observing.

In other words, participate fully. Record as much as possible. When requested, give feedback; do not tune out or sulk, as this closes communication. Clarify and confirm whether you do or do not understand. Confirming: what people understand to be a form of affirmation.

RESISTANCE TO GIVE: PAINFUL FEARS GENERATE FEEDBACK THAT WE WILL BE WRONG, INACCURATE, OR CENTERED OUT.

Paradigmatic anxiety arises when there is an attempt to deny, defend, or distort our belief system.

How do we feel about the three do's of communication? When we communicate, have we used this method consciously?

THE THREE DON'TS OF COMMUNICATION

When communicating with others, always be aware of the three don'ts of communication. There are conflicting situations when people have used one or all of the three DON'TS of communication.

1. DON'T DENY

- Don't deny experiences.

- Don't deny the experience of others, especially if it differs.

- Don't deny feelings.

Don't avoid excuses by denying that people have experienced invalidation or collusion (e.g., we do not say or do anything when confronted with racism or sexism.)

Don't deny feelings about our experiences. Don't be deflected by denying the examples of affirmation, invalidation, collusion, racism, and sexism experienced by others.

Don't focus on attempting to prove that the experiences of others are wrong because they differ.

BE CONSCIOUS OF EFFECTIVE COMMUNICATION!

Don't judge the experiences and feelings of others, insisting, since the experience is different, that their experience is now invalid.

IN EFFECTIVE COMMUNICATION, ONE MUST NEVER DENY THE VALIDITY OF THE EXPERIENCE AS INVALIDATING, BASED ON DIFFERENCES IN PERCEPTION, PARADIGMS, OR INTERPRETATION OF THE SIGNIFICANCE OF RACE, COLOUR, SEX, AGE, NATIONAL ORIGIN, RELIGION, CULTURE, LANGUAGE, ETC…

Example: A widower, who is eighty and retired, complains to his son about an invalidating experience with several local merchants. The widower complains that a store omitted one of the bags of groceries that he purchased. He says they told him that "Old people like him were always forgetting their packages," and that it was his fault. The man's son says that he has never experienced such a thing at the store, and that his father must be mistaken.

HOW IS THIS INEFFECTIVE COMMUNICATION?

He does not realize that by denying his father's experience, he has closed communication channels.

Our parents or guardians are so accustomed to this form of behavior. When children explain how they are depressed, some parents will automatically deny the child's feelings, telling them that they are spoiled compared to when they, the parents, were young. They tell them how lucky they are these days —that they have it good.

EXPLAIN OUR EXPERIENCES

I once had an experience at school where I felt that one of the teachers was very racist and treated me differently from the other students, who were white. For a long time, people did not know what it was, so they mentioned it to a counselor, who indicated that it must be their attitude, and that it has nothing to do with color. The counselor denied the experience when people said that it had nothing to do with race or religion. The result of this is ineffective communication.

Don't deny your feelings about your experiences. Don't be deflected by denying the examples of affirmation, invalidation, collusion, racism, and sexism experienced by others.

Don't focus on attempting to prove that the experiences of others are wrong because they differ.

When this is about to happen, always perform an affirmation, and observe the behavioral response.

When people feel compelled to deny or attack the experience of others, based on race, sex, or age, this feeling is a paradigmatic barrier. Paradigmatic anxiety is when people attempt to conceal, deny, or defend.

2. DON'T DEFEND

- Don't use habitual excuses and cover stories.

- Don't use *"yeah but"* defenses.

- Don't become your position in defense of it. Don't avoid experiencing GET R.E.A.L. by focusing on defenses or feeling attacked by every statement and excuse. They do not have to agree; we must agree to disagree, to seek understanding.

Always be open and courageous, and don't defend or cover up painful feelings. Don't take the victim stance—when we take the victim stance, or respond defensively, this is considered a weak position for effective communication.

E.g., "Yeah, but I am modest, I do not see myself as beautiful."

"Yeah, but black people are racist too."

Don't try to prove that you are right by saying, "Yeah, but you said to do it this way; I heard you." Or, "Yeah, but they did not tell me to clean up my whole room; they just said to hang up my things." Or, "Yeah, but it was not sexist; I use the same tone with everybody."

When we defend, it prevents people from listening, understanding, and experiencing the feeling. When this happens, people use a sense of humor as an intervention. Instead of focusing on defenses, focus on affirmation, intervention, and personal power. Take a proactive approach.

THE GET R.E.A.L. APPROACH

Don't use war stories as your life story—this is an ineffective approach.

3. DON'T DISTORT

- Don't project invalidating judgements.
- Don't project motives unto others.
- Don't distort events and relationships.

Don't invalidate your ability to understand or your ability to write. Respond in a GET R.E.A.L. manner; it is essential not to distort experiences by projecting motives.

Example: When people feel invalidated by a teacher, they have feelings or theories about why the teacher is invalidating them(racism, sexism)—and may mishear vital elements of the event. Don't try to prove people right about the teacher's motives.

It becomes a distorted view—incorrect.

Listen to all the facts. DON'T DISTORT or contradict a point because you feel uncomfortable. Whenever you feel uncomfortable, always listen and observe accurately. You will have R.E.A.L. self-esteem as a result.

THE GET R.E.A.L. CONFLICT RESOLUTION METHOD

STEP 1: RESPECT – TREAT THE OTHER PERSON(S) WITH RESPECT

As human beings, it is tough to treat a person with respect. Respect for one another is an attitude conveyed by specific behaviors. Respect involves the way we listen, how we look at each other, and the tone of our voice. The selection of words and type of reasoning I use either conveys my respect or disrespect.

It is unfortunate when a disagreement with another person's beliefs or values often turns into disrespect for the other person's idea and personhood. It happens even when the person respects the other person. They might disrespect the other person because they feel they may lose the *power and control* of the situation.

Examples:

"What an asshole."

"That's the dumbest thing I have heard in years."

For many of us, an act of willpower is needed to fight the gravitational pull into disrespect. GET R.E.A.L. is required in order to treat the other as they deserve, with whom we will then enter into dialogue as equals.

STEP 2: LISTEN; EXPERIENCE THE OTHER SIDE.

At the best of times, effective communication is difficult to achieve. During a conflict, when feelings are strong, people are usually accurate in their communication. GET R.E.A.L. feels that this is one of the best ways to communicate. GET R.E.A.L. feels that one of the best ways to communicate accurately during disagreements, and to resolve conflict, is for each person to speak up for he/she, but only after he/she has first restated the ideas and feelings of the previous speaker accurately, and to the speaker's satisfaction.

The objective is to understand the content of the other person's ideas or proposals, the meaning it has for him/her, and the feelings he/she has about it. The key is to step into the other person's shoes.

Example:

Mother: "I'm angry because every time I ask you to complete your household chores, you say you cannot because you have to do your homework."

Roddy: (trying to summarize his mother's statement) "You want me to forget about my homework and do the chores?"

Roddy has distorted the meaning of what his mother has said. Effective communication is the answer:

Roddy: "You're upset because you think I use homework as an excuse for not doing my household chores."

When replying, it is Roddy's job to understand, not necessarily to agree.

People need to be understood and accepted.

One of the most common mistakes people make when trying to communicate effectively is to say, "I know how you feel." The other person rarely believes it. Don't offer explanations, apologies, or make any other statements at this point. You must be disciplined to understand the opinions, suggestions, or feelings of the other person.

When the other person feels heard, you have then earned the right to speak your point of view and express your feelings.

STEP 3: STATE VIEWS, NEEDS, FEELINGS

Once you listen to the other person, it is your turn to communicate the meaning to that person. The GET R.E.A.L. process:

1. State your point of view briefly. Keep your message short and to the point.

2. Avoid loaded words. It can be difficult during tense times. Don't use words to act as bombs or bullets.

3. "Say what you mean and mean what you say." State the truth as it is to you.

4. Disclose feelings. Constructively express. Let the other person know how you feel.

5. Analyze the above stage, and use each at the appropriate time. Each step may not apply to every situation.

It is essential to understand that this method is an alternative to violence. This method has no guarantee, due to human interaction (unpredictable).

Take "power and control" of the situation.

Notes

Notes

CHAPTER 3
Paradigms

Definition: model; theory; perception; assumption; frame of reference.

It is the way we see the world, not in the visual sense, but regarding perceiving, understanding, and interpreting.

The Goal

The purpose of this section is to increase the ability to understand, analyze, and diagnose events by transforming unaware perceptions/belief systems, which block effective communication, learning, and teaching.

We intend to become *barrier breakers*.

Why do you cringe and feel your body implode with the intense psychological and emotional changes of the fight or flight response when a person you perceive to be homeless approaches you?

People are so shocked to hear that their fair skinned neighbor is a serial killer. He looked like the all-American kid. The media continuously shows an assortment of photos of what is normal, when their perception is in jeopardy. However, in the media, they take someone of color and perpetuate what are racist attitudes, using the opposite effect. We will see a mug shot, but we will never see his holiday photos or photos with his family, or him as a young child. The media, in those two situations, fulfills the perception of what a murderer looks like. What does a murderer look like?

It is midnight, and you are walking in an underground parking lot. You are approaching the elevator, and you hear someone walking behind you. Your heart starts to beat faster, and you start breathing more rapidly. You get on the elevator, and that person gets on the elevator with you. Describe the person. Is the person big or small? Is it a man or woman? What race are they? Do they have facial hair? Are they young or old? Is it a homeless person or someone of wealth?

The description of the person is a perception of what you have formulated in your mind. A murderer is a murderer. So, why is it easy for us to formulate what a murderer looks like based on ethnicity, race, and gender?

Why do we believe that the religious missionaries that come to our home are the biggest pains in the ass ? Is it because they are purposely trying to disturb and inconvenience us, or is it because they believe in their mission and think their message may help or be important? What we have failed to realize is that they are just doing what they do, every day of their lives.

They are upholding and perpetuating a way of life they have learned to perceive and believe in, being better than or more important than, or stronger than or more fulfilling than, someone else's. Religious missionary paradigm reflects how we perceive them, whether the reaction is to slam the door in their faces be rude and abrupt, or be polite and considerate.

Everything we think and believe about every new experience is what we have learned to understand, interpret, and perceive from our past experiences. The questions we must be responsible and accountable for are:

1. Do you consciously investigate the context of the environment you learn in?

2. Is what you learn based on objective, truthful fact?

The learned perceptions we are conscious of are based on the truth, and reflect responsibility, effectiveness, and affirmation. The learned perceptions that we are not conscious of, and that are not based on the truth, do not. Do you ever question and challenge your beliefs, or do you accept them? The answer to this will tell you if you are R.E.A.L. (Responsible, Effective, Affirmed, Learning) or UNR.E.A.L.

Therefore, we define paradigms as *"how we see the world, not in the visual sense, but regarding perceiving, understanding, and interpreting."* When we fail to examine and investigate, we will automatically rely on previously established beliefs to form a perception, interpretation, and understanding of who, what, or where we are experiencing.

Seeing is believing! Or is it? Many people will tell you that *"seeing is believing."* Don't always trust your sense of sight. We are aware of the things around us because of our senses (sight, smell, touch, hearing, taste), but the perception of these events and objects that fill our life depends on how our brain interprets them.

Exercise:

Pick two people to talk about something. Have them read prepared literature. It is essential to have both of the subjects read at the same time.

Purpose: No one will be able to follow both conversations correctly—only bits and pieces—because our brain will only concentrate on one at a time.

Using sight, we tend to group things that are similar, and separate things that are not. We do this with hairstyles, skin tones, physical features, and language. When we group things, we eventually become lazy, and we guess, assume, and fill in space with our own perceived solution. As individuals, we do this with many things, including literature.

Example: How many Fs do you see in the following sentence? Don't overthink it and don't spend a lot of time on it.

"Finished files are the result of years of scientific study combined with the experience of years."

Answer: Most people say three but the answer is six. Most people don't count the fs in three "of s".

Though we are generally able to perceive the world in a way that allows us to live quite successfully, it is not difficult to get the brain to perceive the world falsely.

Examples, such as above, help us to understand that perception is not specific or innate. We *see* things based on predictions that we make from experience. In general, we make the best bet we can, on what we have learned, and the information that our senses provide. Our ability to perceive the world seems to be learned.

Illusions are defined as any perception that doesn't agree with objective measurements or observations. They produce errors in perception that cause us to develop a false impression of the facts presented to our senses.

Examples:

Hallucinations should not be confused with illusions. A hallucination is an object, figure, design, or some other mental image of which we are consciously aware, but which does not arise from stimulation of the senses.

External stimulation does not cause this.

Example: an alcoholic who sees *pink elephants* or *giant ants*.

Individuals are often unaware of specific major invalidating belief systems or paradigms learned early in life.

Examples of paradigms people are unaware of:

Invalidating (UNR.E.A.L.) paradigm and affirmative (R.E.A.L.) paradigms: invalidation, insults, humiliation, diminishment of freedom, justice, equality, and dignity. An UNR.E.A.L. paradigm is an unaware, negative perception that controls a person's attitude towards something.

Example:

- "Women are born to follow, while men are born to lead."
- "Men are intellectual; women are emotional."
- "Blonde hair is more beautiful than *kinky* hair."
- "Fat people are unattractive."
- "Racism and sexism are just human nature."

In most cases, individuals deny, distort, or even defend their statement with responses:

- "Racism does not exist anymore." "I do not see color."
- "Equal opportunity exists for all."

If most individuals did not think about or believe invalidating racist, sexist, or other elitist paradigms, then:

People would NOT ask…

- Where is it *okay* to live, work, or vacation?
- Who is *okay* to select as a date, husband, wife, friend, or role model.
- Which beauty salon, barber shop, or hairstyle is *okay*?

- Which school is *okay* to attend?

TRANSFORMING UNR.E.A.L. PARADIGMS TO R.E.A.L. PARADIGMS

When transforming UNR.E.A.L. paradigms to R.E.A.L. paradigms, one must not take part in:

- Put-downs or jokes about others

- Racial, ethnic, or cultural conflicts

- Sexual harassment

- Substance abuse

- The inability to affirm oneself and others

Example:

A woman was being harassed with inappropriate, erotic language, sexist jokes, and sexual overtures by a male manager in her company.

The woman intervenes affirmatively by reporting the incident to the president of the company. She asks that the harassment stop, before more severe action is taken, which might impact the company's reputation and the manager's reputation.

In this way, the woman begins the transformation of the invalidating sexist environment. The environment has to change, or it will show that it condones sexist jokes and sexual harassment.

Regardless of the outcome, the woman has maximized her self-confidence and self-esteem through her courageous act—she got **R.E.A.L.**

Responsible * **E**ffective * **A**ffirmed * **L**earning/Living

What would you do, based on the following?

People around you start telling racial jokes about a new girl in your neighborhood/school.

You were informed not to travel to one part of town because it supposedly consists of low-class citizens.

It is a cold day, and there is no parking left in the mall parking lot except for the spots designated for the handicapped.

When examining UNR.E.A.L. paradigms, it is essential to understand the basis of the paradigm—paradigms as a *safety net.*

An examined belief system and frames of references are R.E.A.L. paradigms.

The individual's social experience is *"determined and delimited by the way in which he/she interprets and responds to the conflict of UNR.E.A.L. paradigms."*

SAFETY NET PARADIGMS

We use *safety net* paradigms to remind us not to make the same mistake twice.

Example: In a lifetime, we have experimented with temperature, height, weight, etc.If we touch something that is hot, we get burned. If we jump off something high, we can get hurt. Even though there are safety net paradigms, individuals continue to challenge something that they have already experienced negatively.

Examples:

- Drinking and Driving
- Substance Abuse

THE POWER OF A PARADIGM

Have individuals try a pair of glasses on (different types)—dark, light, bifocals, progressives—for nearsightedness or farsightedness.

Have individuals look at an object and explain what they see. Each will see something different with regards to perception. The individual will question what they see as not being accurate.

Purpose: This exercise indicates that the individuals who are wearing the glasses will question what they see because they can take off the glasses to see the truth. In real life, we seldom question a paradigm's accuracy (we assume).

People see the same thing but with a different unique lens experience. People must take off the glasses and examine the vision. The *pair of glasses theory* affects our perceptions.

Few seconds vs. lifetime of conditioning:

The *pair of glasses theory* controls our attitude and behavior. People respond when the glasses are taken off: "Really? Aha! No way! Wow, I do not believe it!"

Example: At one time, individuals took for granted that the world was flat, and that there was an end, where explorers could fall off. A few explorers questioned this theory and carefully examined the *flat world perception.*

Final result = world is round.

Think about inventions. Explain how they made a *Paradigm Shift.*

1) **Bus ride home**

A man was on a bus with his children. The children ranged from ages 4 to 10 years. They were very loud and rambunctious. People were sitting very quietly in the car, but seemed to be very disturbed about the children acting out of control. The people looked at the man, who just closed his eyes as if he did not care.

As a passenger, what would you do in this case?

Paradigm shift—A person in the subway car eventually approaches the man and asks him if he could do something about his children, who are disturbing everyone. He explains that they just came back from the hospital, where their mother died about an hour ago.

2) **Bigger Boat**

A battleship was assigned to sea maneuvers in heavy weather for several days. The visibility was poor, with patchy fog. Shortly after dark, the captain of the battleship remained on the bridge. The captain noticed a light through the fog. He directed the signal officer to signal the ship to indicate that they were on a collision course. A signal came back, advising the captain to change his course 20 degrees. The captain told the signal officer to signal that he was a captain, and would not change his course. A signal came back, saying, "I'm a seaman, second class, and you better change your course."

What would you do if you were the captain?

Paradigm Shift—The captain was furious and directed the signal officer to reply: "I am a battleship." A signal came back: "I am a lighthouse."

3) **Sunday afternoon drive**

A man was taking his regular Sunday afternoon drive in the country. Everything was the same as every other Sunday. The man memorized every bump and bend in the road. He could drive the road blindfolded. He was approaching his favorite bend in the road when he suddenly saw a car driving out of control towards him. The car drove past him, and a lady yelled out, "PIG!"

What would you do?

Paradigm Shift—The man was very confused by this and responded by giving the lady the finger. He told himself that the lady was driving drunk and was going to hurt someone. As he came upon his favorite bend in the road, a pig was in the middle of the road. The car went out of control and went over the cliff.

How do you feel now?

Exercise:

Q. A boy and girl are born on the same day, same month, same year, to the same parents, and they are not twins.

A. They were two of triplets.

Q. If it takes six days to dig six holes, how long will it take one man to dig half a hole?

A. There is no such thing as half a hole. A hole is a hole.

Explain.

Q. Thompson and his men searched the tundra for the escaped convict, Shadow. Just as they were about to give up, one of Thompson's men spotted a body. Shadow was found lying dead in the snow. No tracks were leading to or from the body. The cause of death was partially due to the unopened pack on his back. Shadow did not die of thirst, hunger, or cold. What was in Shadow's pack that lead to his death?

A. An unopened parachute.

Society has become extremely lazy and misinformed of the world we know, and the world we do not know. Although most are generally able to perceive the world in a way that allows them to live successfully, it is common to develop and trust false perceptions. We often *see* new things based on assumptions and predictions from old experiences. When we do this, we are making our best possible bet, based on what we have already learned. When we choose to be lazy our perception, understanding, and interpretation are dependent on this process. When we do not take the time to be responsible, effective, and affirmed by examining and investigating that which we experience, we are choosing to be lazy. We frequently rely on the laziness of assumption, but do we ever consider the limitations it poses? Review the following statements. Do you believe any of them?

- Men are intellectual; women are emotional.

- Straight hair is more beautiful than dark, kinky hair.

- Racism and sexism is just human nature.

- Kids are too young to know what love is.

- Welfare recipients or poor people do nothing but drink and smoke crack.

- Stop trying to change the world, because it is not going to change.

These represent a fraction of the irresponsible, ineffective, and unaffirmed paradigms that control our beliefs. For them to have become established truths, they should have been consciously examined and investigated, questioned and challenged, but they were not. By questioning and challenging such paradigms, we can reveal the standards and expectations that will enable us to prove them as truth or disprove them as false assumptions.

Many of us do not do this because we never learned to do so. We have been conditioned to accept and believe many things that are not representative of the truth. Paradigms of this nature are not irresponsible, ineffective, and unaffirmed. They are UNR.E.A.L. when we allow them to be governed by UNR.E.A.L. paradigms, and we find ourselves reacting negatively to a standard or expectation that has not been examined and investigated. We define UNR.E.A.L. paradigms as *"unaware, unconscious negative perceptions that control a person's attitude towards someone or something."* UNR.E.A.L. paradigms ensure that we will react to people and situations, because we do not choose to question or challenge such beliefs. Our family, our friends, our community, our country, and our world have negative perceptions that govern our behavior because we have accepted them as being the truth. When we affirm, we can proclaim ourselves to be "just as beautiful, just as intelligent, just as sensual as…"

If not, your paradigm regarding yourself is UNR.E.A.L. because you have not questioned and challenged society's standards and expectations of beauty, intelligence and sensuality. If you had, you would have understood they are not true.

There is a way to conquer the laziness produced by UNR.E.A.L. paradigms. To do so, we must go back and question and challenge everything we have learned. It does not mean everything we have learned is not the truth. It means that everything should be. Society, the term we use to represent everyone and everything apart from oneself (i.e., your parents, friends, relatives, teachers, employers, the media, public institutions), has conditioned you to form paradigms based on the perception and assumption of truth, not objective facts. If society had not done this, we would not believe any UNR.E.A.L. paradigm statements concerning beauty, intelligence, and sensuality, because they would not exist. When we choose to question and challenge UNR.E.A.L. paradigms, we must do so at the point where the conditioning takes place, and the information is a change from objective fact to a perception of the truth.

To help understand this conditioning process, let us use an illustrated analogy. Consider the information concerning every aspect of society—age, gender, sexuality, race, language, beauty, intelligence, sensuality, religion, safety (sex, violence, and substance abuse), socioeconomic status, political platform—is contained in a bottle. Imagine that you are a newborn baby who needs to learn this information to understand how society wants you, as a newborn, to learn its version of the truth—society is going to feed you the contents of the bottle. You want that information to be the truth, because you would want that information to be accurate, and because you do not want to believe something that isn't true.

We need to challenge and question the world in order to live as a responsible, effective, and affirmed person. Therefore, the best way to learn that information is to drink and digest all the information in the bottle. By doing this, we would guarantee that what we believe about those individual aspects of society would be on R.E.A.L. paradigms. Everything we learned about society would be based on the truth. However, this is not the socialization or type of learning process we indeed experienced, because elitist society beliefs are based on the truth of humanity.

What happened is that before we drank and digested the truthful, fact-based information from the bottle, we poured it, through a filter, into another bottle containing our paradigms. If we compare the information in the bottle of society, with that in the bottle of our paradigms, we would see disparaging differences. The filter often changes the nature of the information because not all of it may get transferred from bottle to bottle. The result are paradigms that may not have all the facts or the whole story. The filter may condition the information of age, gender, safety, race, language, beauty, intelligence, or sensuality—paradigms of age, and gender roles/ stereotypes, fashion, smart vs. stupid, racism, sexism, and other forms of elitism. Any paradigm not based on the truth is UNR.E.A.L. However, this does not mean all paradigms are UNR.E.A.L. Discovering the difference challenges everything we have learned about society. To do this responsibly, effectively, and in an affirmed manner, we must go back to the point where the filter affects the information. The filter is the media, and the effect is its manipulation of information on our beliefs.

Every time we question and challenge our beliefs, or those of someone else, we will begin to establish R.E.A.L. paradigms. We define R.E.A.L. paradigms as, *"consciously examined and investigated perceptions that expand a person's power of positive intervention."* This decisive intervention is our search for an understanding of the truth. It is this decisive intervention that will enable us to think and live proactively. If we are not willing to make a conscious effort to intervene and find the truth, we should not be willing to believe in and be controlled by paradigms that are UNR.E.A.L.

Notes

Notes

CHAPTER 4
What is R.E.A.L. Self-Esteem?

"Self-esteem is the reputation we acquire with ourselves."

—Nathaniel Branden

Before understanding self-esteem, one must have a foundation or starting point. Picture the construction of a 15-story building. The most critical part of the building is the foundation because it secures the building from crumbling to the ground. In this case, the building represents your self-esteem. As a result, the word, *self-esteem*, means different things to different people. The word *self-esteem* is one of the most loosely used words to describe a result of something. Ask anyone what self-esteem is, and they will tell you several meanings, such as how you feel about yourself, or confidence. People use the word, *self-esteem*, when speaking of an accomplishment, such as losing weight or winning at something. "I lost 50 lbs., and my self-esteem improved."

The above statements are all true; however, we must add one component to all the meanings, before the actual definition is complete. Instead of calling it just *self-esteem*, we will call it R.E.A.L. self-esteem.

Think of that person who has a positive self-affirmation, which means they look at their beauty, sensuality, and intelligence without comparison, qualification, or reservation. Think of that person who has vision, exploration, no fear, no limits, and humility. That person is a 1 to 2½-year-old child.

We come into this world as a being that has no limits. We are told immediately how beautiful, how intelligent and sensual we are, with no comparison or reservation. We look in the mirror and smile at skin tucked into our diaper. We celebrate our body as we run around the house naked. Everyone who sees us tells us how beautiful we are. We see the difference but embrace it. We look at a dog or cat as our equal. We do not know what judgment is until our parents tell us, or television and our assimilation into the outside world.

The toddler gates that are put up in a house are put up in the outside world as well. For example, a toddler is taken to the park for the first time, and he/she sees other toddlers. The other toddlers could be another race or culture, and the parent immediately reacts by tugging or pulling the toddler back from playing with those who are different. A toddler sees a difference but doesn't feel superior or inferior. The parent starts setting up toddler gates everywhere, and thinks they are doing it to keep the toddler safe, but in fact, they are creating a division. They dress the toddler in what is thought to be gender appropriate and buy them toys that are gender specific. Those gates intend to provide safety, but at the same time, it imprisons their development.

A toddler is praised for everything they do, and it is preached to them that they can be anything they want to be. The irony is that later in life, they decide to do something different than what they were told. Once again, the toddler gate is put up. "You cannot do that. What will people say?"

We can learn a lot by looking through the eyes of a toddler.

What does an affirmation paradigm have to with self-esteem?

Affirmation of yourself serves a fulcrum of the GET R.E.A.L. program because everything revolves around it. The key is planting the seed of R.E.A.L. self-esteem. We need to understand R.E.A.L. self-esteem. Once we understand that, we will be able to move to the next step, which is understanding how to nurture R.E.A.L. self-esteem. It is like a newly planted seed: it must be watered and fertilized in order to take root, sprout, and blossom, and eventually bear fruit. The fruit will be harvested from well-nurtured, R.E.A.L. self-esteem,

R.E.A.L. communication leads to R.E.A.L. leadership once we reach this level , we do not automatically stay there. Maximized self-esteem is something that needs nurturing because, every day of our life, our self-esteem will be questioned and challenged. R.E.A.L. self-esteem is a lifestyle choice —an acquired awareness—not a quick fix or Band-Aid solution. R.E.A.L. self-esteem must be an experience based on our ability to affirm.

Without self-affirmation experiences, we will not correctly nurture our R.E.A.L. self-esteem and, subsequently, our communication leadership will be limited. We feel the meaning of self-esteem has become stored, and because of this, its importance has become trivialized. Therefore, it is imperative to establish a definition for self-esteem. If we consider the two words separately, we will notice that *self* is how we see our *self* and others.

Pride, confidence, success, accomplishment, and achievement are a manifestation of social standards and expectations. We learned this during our lifelong socialization process. We learned at the dinner table, on the playground, and in the media. It is society-esteem, not self-esteem. Let us put a value on or have esteem for something that is not our humanity; we give up ownership of our self-esteem. Many people feel good and proud of themselves because of what they own, whom they know, what they do, and what they have accomplished or achieved. These are not indicative of self-esteem, because they are not *self*. When people do this, they are desperately trying to fulfill their sense of belonging. We should not allow such things to be the basis of our self-esteem. What happens when we lose our possessions, or we do not reach our target accomplishment? Does the esteem we have for our humanity suffer? For many, the answer is yes, and that is a sad commentary about how society operates. *"There is nothing in the rule book that says an elephant cannot play baseball."*

One day, I was discussing with a friend the many different situations he had experienced where people have said things that are supposed to portray the rules in which society operates on accurately. Suddenly, he blurted out, "There's nothing in the rule book that says an elephant cannot play baseball; so play ball!" I looked at him as if to say, "Where did that come from, and what are you talking about?" Then he broke out laughing. He explained that he quoted the saying, or paraphrased from a cartoon, in which an elephant begins playing baseball and wins the big game. The game was protested by the opposition, saying that elephants cannot play baseball. The umpire reviewed the rulebook and stated that there is nothing in the rulebook about an elephant playing baseball.

Our approach to maximizing self-esteem on a R.E.A.L. level is an individual's ability to affirm their humanity unconditionally. We must be able to shift our paradigm about ourselves, by affirming our beauty, intelligence, and sensuality, before we can begin to shift the other paradigms that may control our lives. We cannot emphasize enough that if we have not experienced self-affirmation to this point, we will be unable to move on properly. The ability to transcend the limits that society has conditioned us to believe is what our R.E.A.L. self-esteem will mean. The example of the elephant playing baseball may be out of place or ridiculous, but what is truly ridiculous is that we may not believe we are a beautiful, intelligent, and sensual human beings. Believing anything else is indignant and disrespects oneself. How then can we expect to be able to respect and dignify others?

We define self-esteem as the self, or image of the self, as defined by an individual's paradigm. Self-esteem is what one believes about oneself. Overall, our belief is the truth, or a distorted version of it.

One of our favorite resources, but one we also hate the most, is the annual edition of *People Magazine's 50 Most Beautiful People in the World* publication. Every time we use it, we ask participants in our sessions the following questions:

- Are you as beautiful as they are?

- What makes you less beautiful than them?

- Why aren't you as beautiful as them?

- Why isn't your picture included?

- How can there be 50 people in this world of over 7 billion that are more beautiful than anyone else?

Do you understand that young women are starving themselves to death because they are trying to be something or someone they cannot be, and who does not even exist?

The sad realization is that this only challenges one aspect of self-esteem. What happens when intelligence and sensuality are jeopardized? There are increases in suicide, dropout rates, violence, criminal activity, substance use and abuse, and eating disorders.

When people turn to these types of solutions for answers, they are exhibiting low and UNR.E.A.L. levels of self-esteem. We define low self-esteem as, *"the self or image of the self as defined by the UNR.E.A.L. paradigm demonstrated through the invalidation of self."* Anytime we do something or become involved in an activity that jeopardizes our humanity because we invalidate ourselves, we are indicating we have low self-esteem. Invalidation refers to anything that defines insult, humiliation, patronization, and the diminishment of freedom, justice, equality, and dignity. If we are not able to affirm ourselves, we have low self-esteem. What can we do about it?

When we do not feel good about ourselves, because we have a poor self-image, we can make ourselves feel better and improve our self-image by invalidating someone else. It means we believe we are more beautiful, more intelligent, and more sensual than others. It is indicative of UNR.E.A.L. self-esteem because it is not responsible, effective, or affirming to believe we are better than somebody else. It is not the truth; it is only a perception—what makes someone's humanity better or more important than someone else's? We define UNR.E.A.L. self-esteem as *"the self or image of the self as defined by the UNR.E.A.L. paradigm demonstrated through the invalidation of others."* This takes the focus away from the truth of your humanity and the humanity of others.

If we want to make our self-esteem R.E.A.L., then we must focus on our self —on our humanity. We must be able to question and challenge any paradigm that jeopardizes our self, as defined by the R.E.A.L. paradigm demonstrated through the validation of self and others. Only as an affirmed individual will you have R.E.A.L. self-esteem and survive those challenges.

THE SELF-FULFILLING PROPHECY

The self-fulfilling prophecy is one of those classic edicts that echo through our society. It means that we will become what we think or believe about ourselves every minute of every day. If you have UNR.E.A.L. paradigms (low or UNR.E.A.L. self-esteem), then you will live reactively and unaware of what is going on around you, but if you can make that shift and change the foundation of your beliefs to R.E.A.L. paradigms (R.E.A.L. self-esteem), you will begin to live proactively and be conscious of everything you say, read, hear, and do. It will determine whether you are fulfilling a R.E.A.L. self-esteem prophecy or an UNR.E.A.L. or low self-esteem prophecy. Before I explain self-fulfilling prophecy, you must know the three elements that make and drive your self-esteem.

The first of three is self-identity, which is defined as, *"how we choose to distinguish ourselves in each context."* Too many of us use our successes, accomplishments, achievements, possessions, or friends as identities. The problem with this approach is that they are not *self*. If a person who identifies themselves in this way loses these things, or does not accomplish these things, does that mean they lose their identity or cease to exist? The answer, for many people, is yes. Our identity should begin with our affirmation. What we do, who we know, and what we have accomplished should confirm who we are, not be the basis for it. This identity is also important in social settings. Do we express our own beliefs and opinions, or do we adopt the beliefs and opinions of others? Do we challenge opinions that offend us or do not seem to be *right*, or do we agree with them because we do not seem to be *right*, and do not feel our opinions are credible?

The second element is self-concept. We define this as, *"how we think others perceive us within a given context."* One of the most influential factors affecting how we feel about our *self* is what we think others think and feel about us. Some people talk negatively and invalidate others whom they feel are *insecure* or *attention seeking*. Why shouldn't those who have never affirmed themselves feel that way when society thrives and survives on judgment, categorization, and separation of people according to beauty, intelligence, and sensuality?

The third element is self-awareness, and we define this as, *"the conscious examination and investigation of yourself in each context."* This means whether or not you are aware of the information your senses are transmitting to your brain at all times. It includes everything we hear, smell, touch, taste, and see. Our senses are receiving information, all the time, and the critical question is whether we are conscious of it or not. Are we aware of the invalidating nature of the UNR.E.A.L. paradigms that are affecting and controlling how we perceive, interpret, and understand ourselves and the rest of society?

Every time we say or do something, we fulfill one of the prophecies. Whether we are aware of it or not, we either choose to have the identity, self-concept, and self-awareness that interacts in such a way that defines our self-esteem as being low, UNR.E.A.L., or R.E.A.L.

When we fulfill the low or UNR.E.A.L. self-esteem prophecy, we identify ourselves with behaviors, attitudes, or beliefs that invalidate our*selves* or someone else.

When we choose not to question any form of invalidation, we send out the message that the behavior, attitude, or belief is acceptable. This behavior is precisely what collusion is. By remaining silent, we aid and abet any invalidation that is happening around us. In the eyes of the law, aiding and abetting a criminal or a criminal activity is the same as committing the crime.

Have you ever failed to question someone when they drive while impaired, or when they tell a joke that insults, humiliates, patronizes, or jeopardizes someone's freedom, dignity, justice, and equality? Have you ever failed to question someone about a problem that may jeopardize his own health and welfare? Have you ever considered yourself to be ugly, unattractive, gross, stupid, or unimportant? Have you ever told someone that they are ugly, unattractive, gross, stupid or that they are unimportant? If you have, then you are fulfilling the low and UNRE.A.L. self-esteem prophecy, because you identified yourself as being better or less than someone else. We have identified ourselves with behaviors and beliefs, which do not promote freedom, dignity, justice, or equality for ourselves or others. The importance of this can make you understand the impact this may have on you or others if we invalidate someone who is not affirmed and is insecure as a result. We may devastate that person.

Do we question jokes that are invalidating? Do we intervene when someone wants to drive impaired? Do we question people when they label themselves or others with such terms as ugly, unattractive, gross, stupid, or unimportant? Do we question people when they make fun of the way others choose to dress, act, or think? If we do, we are fulfilling the R.E.A.L. self-esteem prophecy, because we are using our power of decisive intervention to question and challenge paradigms that may not be R.E.A.L. When we decide to question and challenge, we are asking ourselves, and others, to be accountable and responsible for what we hear, do, and believe. It is merely asking them to take ownership of their beliefs.

It is the fulfillment of these prophecies that will nurture, fertilize, and maintain our self-esteem, but are we going to take ownership and make our self-esteem R.E.A.L, or continue floundering between invalidating ourselves and others? We know the truth, but it is up to us to do something about it. Affirm yourself.

Notes

Notes

CHAPTER 5

Types of Self-Esteem

Because self-esteem manifests itself as having different levels or conditions, it is crucial to express each one in the context of a definition.

- R.E.A.L. Esteem (Maximum)

- Low Self-Esteem

- UNR.E.A.L. Esteem (Pseudo)

Each of these levels or conditions of self-esteem can be identified by observing and targeting verbal and body language character of all three. The following diagrams list some examples of these forms of language, as well as some physiological reactions that may be evident when an individual is experiencing a particular level or condition of self-esteem.

R.E.A.L. SELF-ESTEEM SEESAW

The following diagrams illustrate either balance or imbalance found in an individual's self-esteem, dependent on the level or condition.

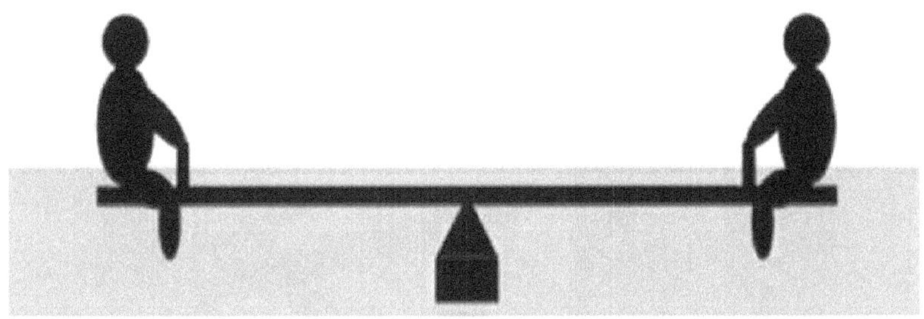

BALANCE AND CENTERED SEESAW

Eye to Eye
Affirmation & Intervention

R.E.A.L. ESTEEM demonstrates a regard for, and association with, the positive paradigm. This individual is affirmed without the presence of collusion or invalidation.

INVALIDATION AND COLLUSION DEPRESS THE SEESAW
(LOW SELF-ESTEEM)

Illustrated regard for, and association with, the negative paradigm about the self. This individual is not affirmed, and collusion and self-invalidation are present.

UNR.E.A.L. AND NONAFFIRMATIVE DEPRESSES THE SEESAW

Pseudo UNR.E.A.L. SELF-ESTEEM-illustrates regard for, and association with, the negative paradigm about the self. This individual is non-affirmed, and the invalidation of others is present.

R.E.A.L. AWARENESS

R.E.A.L. awareness is the awareness of one's own self, and about situations involving the socialization process or moments of solitude. An individual's self-awareness, similar to self-esteem, can be measured, being a positive or negative condition. Therefore, the definition of R.E.A.L. awareness is the conscious ability to examine and inform one's self within a given context or situation.

Having an awareness of self comes from the ability to investigate and examine, through the process of visualization, the condition of the *self*, at any time. The condition of the self directly correlates to, 1) The condition of self-esteem, and 2) What *pair of glasses* they are wearing. Therefore, this awareness is dependent on the ability of an individual to objectively analyze themselves within a given context or situation. It is essential that individuals be able to translate the condition or level of their self-esteem, into both the maintenance and the actualization of the self. It is as though, in the practice of self-awareness, that individuals can recognize the need for an intervention of self-esteem building and paradigm changing strategies. Self-awareness will allow people to realize the condition of their self-esteem, and *change their glasses*. This conscious awareness will allow individuals to use strategies involving affirmation and intervention to regain balance and control of their self-esteem (i.e., R.E.A.L. self-esteem).

Scenario 1

- A child suffering from low self-esteem tries to make him /herself feel better by invalidating others; and then, finally, through the proper interpretation of self-awareness, comes to use affirmative intervention to maximize (R.E.A.L.) self-esteem.

Scenario 2

- Sally fails a math test. Karen, an overweight girl in Sally's math class, is an A student. Sally does not feel good about herself because of her current performance. Sally begins to make fun of

Karen's weight problem. Sally goes from low self-esteem to pseudo self-esteem by invalidating Karen.

SELF-IDENTITY

Every individual has a need and a desire to be recognized in one way or another. It is the struggle to establish an identity which leads people to become involved in activities and associations. As a result, individuals may find themselves engulfed in endeavors that do not enable them to find what they are searching for.

People restrict themselves by choosing to identify themselves through associations or occupations falsely. When people establish their self-identity about their job, or some group or organization they are members of, they ultimately limit the scope of who they are. What people have chosen for a career, or whom they associate with, should only be a reflection of who they are; it should not consume who they are.

People should strive to create their own identity because their self-identity, defined as how they choose to distinguish themselves, is dependent on the affirmation process. It is the realization of affirmation that genuinely creates self-identity. The affirmation within an individual is R.E.A.L. When an individual experiences affirmation and strives for actualization, it is done without comparison to other individuals or things.

Remember, affirmation never refers to an individual being superior /inferior to, or more/less than another living thing. Individuals who use occupations or associations to establish their self-identity will eventually come to compare themselves with other individuals in the workplace or organization. When this happens, people surrender their sense of belonging and ownership to others. This sets people up for using the *victim stance*. This is not responsible, effective, affirmed living.

There are two essential sources when establishing self-identity. The first is that self-identity is equivalent to, and based on, the affirmation process. Only when a person affirms him/herself can they begin to realize and understand what their identity is. Secondly, the establishment of one's self-identity is contextual and, therefore, about situations and personal experiences. In the definition of self-identity, the terms, context, situation, and affirmation begins with the self. It soon transcends the individual to include the appropriate elements of the environment as they pertain to the context of the situation.

Scenarios

- Rick McCarthy is a 17-year-old Canadian of European descent, who lives in a subsidized housing development in the city. He is in grade 12 and is actively involved in sports. He plays basketball, hockey, rugby, and football. Rick also volunteers for a few charitable organizations in his neighborhood.

- Wendy Smith is a 14-year-old Canadian of Trinidadian descent, who lives in a middle-class, suburban neighborhood. She is in grade 9 and is an active participant in the high school theatre arts program. Wendy paints and sings, and she works at Subway during her spare time.

What are the identities for both Rick and Wendy? Do these tell us who they are?

Prepare a list of possible identities that can be used to distinguish yourself from others.

SELF-CONCEPT

Self-concept is the culminating product of self-awareness and self-identity as they reflect on self-esteem. If self-awareness is an individual's conscious ability to examine and inform him/herself according to a defined context or situation, and self-identity is an individual's conscious choice of how to distinguish him/herself according to a defined context or situation, then self-concept is the resulting perception an individual has of themselves.

Therefore, the definition of self-concept is:

> *The general notion of how we see/perceive ourselves within a defined context or situation.*

It is also stated in a formula:

> *Self-Concept =*
> *Self-Awareness x Self-Identity +Self-Awareness =*
> *Self-Concept x Self-Identity+Self-Identity =*
> *Self-Concept x Self-Awareness*

When the definition is written as a mathematical formula that can be manipulated, it is easy to see the relationship and interdependence that exist between the three.

Notes

Notes

CHAPTER 6
Society-Esteem

Any time you feel you must lose 10 pounds, tone up, get drunk or stoned, dye your hair, skip school, invalidate someone, get a hairpiece, challenge a safety net paradigm, use violence to try to demonstrate power control over a situation, buy a new car, buy a bigger car or a more beautiful home, or invalidate yourself or someone else, you have allowed society's expectations and standards to overwhelm you. Society takes over our ownership of our self-esteem. We fulfill society-esteem because we choose to recognize standards and expectations rather than humanity. It is not uncommon. This is what we are conditioned to do through the media's manipulation of information.

Every opportunity society offers in the form of accomplishment, possessions, and association should confirm who we are and what we do. We should not affirm ourselves through them. When we make decisions to partake in activities, friendships/relationships, or associations, we should choose them because they reflect what we believe in and how we feel about ourselves. In short, we should be responsible, effective, and affirmed.

Question:

If our money, clothing, house, car(s), job, or anything else we use to identify ourselves were to be taken away, and driven into a field in the middle of nowhere, would you know who you are?

Think about this, and answer honestly.

CELL YOUR SOUL TO THE DEVIL

Think about it for a second, how we (society) have taken the personal touch out of everything we do. Today's world is all about convenience and expedience. Technology has made it possible to do things we only dreamed of in the past.

How we communicate is one of those paradoxical advancements of technology. The more we advance in communication, the more we move beyond the fundamentals of communicating with one another.

We complain about the cell phone, and at the same time, we cannot do without it.

What does the advancement of cell phones have to do with self-esteem?

It is important to note that when referring to cell phones, we are grouping cell phones among all technology. According to researchers, *"we are in the presence of a new paradigm of communication, where cell phones are part of society, in general, and adolescents are not the exception. In that sense, mobile devices create a parallel reality, and come to fill a void typical of that stage of life in which young people question their existence."*

(blog.familytime.io Dario, on Feb 22, 2018, Parental controls and Parenting teens)

What is social media? Originally, social media was used as a platform for communicating. Social media was used as a tool for businesses to market and advertise.

Don't get me wrong; I have a cell phone, and I love it. It is a fantastic tool for managing our day. At times, I am not sure what I would do without it. While growing up, parents and grandparents used to talk about TV the same way I speak about cell phones. They used to say that TV would "wreck my brain," and that "TV would make me stupid." Now, we have evolved from TV to a portable device that that can affect your emotions in seconds. Watch someone scroll through Instagram or Facebook. Observe the emotions that happen while they scroll: happy, sad, mad, excited, funny, inspired. We become an expert on religion, politics, and cultural affairs. We post, repost, tag a post, and perpetuate the endless cycle of gossip.

The cell phone has introduced us to the new age of editing and production. The days of the Polaroid and waiting for a picture to be developed are gone. Now, our photos and stories on social media, for the most part, are edited, filtered and staged. We post pictures of our cars, houses, vacations, and anything new that we obtained—even a girlfriend or boyfriend. We then look for confirmation of our posts, waiting for the likes and views, and if we are lucky, we will get a comment.

How does this affect our self-esteem?

Social media manipulates our thought processes or paradigms. It keeps us lazy and a prisoner to the pressures of society. We give uninvestigated thoughts, make assumptions, and support unfounded facts.

When viewing or browsing social media, a person should be responsible, effective, and affirmed.

An easy exercise to try is to only read or repost anything that makes us feel good about ourselves. This happiness should not come through material things.

Unfollow people who support invalidating thoughts.

Pick up a book and read a chapter whenever you feel a need to go on social media.

Give yourself a time limit. Always ask what you learned from browsing on social media.

Growing up as one of the only black kids in my city, I was always questioning where I truly fit in. I had lots of friends and didn't cause problems, and I was somewhat famous. However, I always felt that I was not beautiful (handsome), based on the messages that society dictated at the time. I did not have blonde hair or blue eyes. I was completely different, and sort of the *odd man out*. No one said I was ugly; however, the messages that the media and society yelled out were, "you are different; you are inferior." In grade 4, I remember wishing I was white. Saturday morning cartoons, commercials, prime time TV, stories or fairy tales, did not include anyone who looked like me, and if they did, it would in a supporting or in the background. It was not until I went to university that I was introduced to diversity.

In the 1990s, I started closely observing well-known magazines that claimed that they had the 50 most beautiful people in their magazine. It featured all TV actors and movies stars, in several posed pictures.

In 1996, the *Hamilton Spectator* published pictures comprising the results of a poll that asked *Harlequin Romance* novel readers what the perfect image of male and female was. Once again, these pictures portrayed white Europeans with straight hair and pronounced sculpted facial features.

Mirabella magazine publishes one of its editions with the cover photo of a woman considered to be the epitome of beauty. The woman has straight hair, and bright, light skin, and pronounced facial features—and the photo is not real. It is a computer-generated composite of features taken from many different sources determined to represent beauty.

Now we move forward 20 years to the explosion of Facebook, Instagram, and Twitter, and their role in the definition of beauty. The term *selfie* is now part of the Webster's dictionary. Photos have been enhanced and are usually filtered and photo-shopped. The issue is not those who are posting but those viewing this unrealistic world, for the most part.

We find these examples, and countless more like them, to be so disturbing they bring us to the brink of physical illness. Every time we come across them, we must ask each other who it was that decided what beauty is, what the perfect face is, and who created the standards and expectations that define them.

Every day, we hear many people say many things that reflect society's belief in the importance of beauty. Some of these include:

"I was looking at everyone last night, and half the people there were hideous. I mean, ugly."

"I am one of those people who don't look good unless I have makeup on."

"Oh, my god! She is fat and gross; she should not be wearing that outfit."

"You would look so much better if you grew your hair."

"You have lost so much weight; I cannot get over how great you look now."

"There's a guy who lives in the same building. He is on welfare. I do not know if he is trying to get off it or what. It is too bad, because he is young and good looking."

These comments were made either directly or indirectly to us by people from varying walks of life. They show that the concept of beauty is significant, and what it means is universal, and has a particular impact on how we perceive others. What is problematic about these comments and their underlying beliefs is that to find out where they come from simply turn on the TV, read a magazine or book, or look at Facebook. Instantly we will notice the separation between beautiful and ugly in the media.

"I lost 25 lbs in one month, and I look great and feel great."

"It is so nice to see spring coming with its bright colors, because now women can be beautiful again."

"Revealing the beauty tips of the world's supermodels."

"The fifty most beautiful people in the world."

"Not only did my hairpiece make me look better, it gave me higher self-esteem."

These messages are not subliminal; they are loud and blatant—right in our face. We get facelifts, tummy tucks, liposuction, breast and penis enlargements; we jump on rollercoaster diets, and use enhancing performance drugs, to be what the media tells us is beautiful.

However, have we ever considered what real beauty is? Have we ever questioned or challenged the standards and expectations that have been placed on us? Have we ever considered who created them or where they came from? Furthermore, have we ever considered what it truly means to be intelligent or sensual? Do we ever wonder why society judges, categorizes, and separates us according to its standards and expectations?

Over the past 25 years of examining self-esteem, I have noticed that the more advanced we have become, the more our self-esteem has diminished. Our self-esteem is *under fire* more today than ever. The Internet has evolved so much that we have become dependent upon it for our validation.

Subliminal messages are no more. The messages we see now are blatant and overt. We carry our computer in our pocket in the form of a cell phone. It dictates to us what is beautiful, intelligent, and sensual.

We have actually "sold our *cell* to the devil." We become stalkers of people to create a romanticized world. We put value in how people look, what they own, whom they know, and what they are doing. We then like and/or share with our friends.

Notes

Notes

CHAPTER 7

"I Was Blind, But Now I Can See"

What should we do when an UNR.E.A.L. paradigm confronts us? We must not take part in it. We must not be a party to any joke, insult, patronization, or humiliation that jeopardizes our humanity or the humanity of another person. We must be able to intervene in a responsible, effective, and affirmed manner, to deal with racist, sexist, or religious conflict, sexual harassment, drug, and alcohol use/abuse, or the inability to affirm ourselves or others. If we do this, we will shift the paradigm from being UNR.E.A.L. to being R.E.A.L.

Why do we say some of the hurtful, rude, indignant, disrespectful, and humiliating things we do? It is because we are lazy and do not consider the impact of what we say, what we think, or how we behave. We never consider that someone may be hurt, offended, disrespected, or humiliated. Because society is based on so many UNR.E.A.L. paradigms, we will quickly rationalize what we say and do by relying on our 3-D glasses. These cause us to *Deny, Distort,* and *Defend* our beliefs, by using expressions such as "that is the reality;" "that is human nature;" "that is just the way it is;" or "that is just common sense." The next time you find yourself rationalizing your beliefs or behaviors in these ways, please stop and ask yourself who it was that decided what reality and human nature are, what is familiar, and who decides that is the way it is. These conditional beliefs only exist if we continue to perpetuate them.

To shift UNR.E.A.L. paradigms about others, we must first shift our paradigm about ourselves, from UNR.E.A.L. to R.E.A.L. If we do not learn and accept the truth about ourselves, how do we expect to learn and accept the truth about others? Believing ourselves to be anything other than beautiful, intelligent, and sensual is UNR.E.A.L. When we do this, we judge, categorize, and separate our self, based on society's UNR.E.A.L. conditional standards and expectations of conformity. Why should we marginalize ourselves and jeopardize our humanity, based on something that is not the truth?

An UNR.E.A.L. paradigm is like a magician on stage, with us in the front row watching the show, eager to believe that everything we see or hear is real. We witness several tricks, some sleight of hand, and someone or something disappearing and then reappearing. We see it and believe it, we clap our hands, and we cheer, but do those things happen the way see them? To find the answer, all we need to do is use the 20-cent (pair of dimes/paradigms) solution: 10 cents for questioning and 10 cents for challenging. We will spend 20 cents every time we choose to try and establish the truth, by questioning and challenging our learning experience. Unless we are watching a magician's performance, we should not allow ourselves to be tricked into believing something that is not based on objective, factual truth.

Safety Net paradigm is another type of paradigm that we want to introduce. Not all paradigms have to be questioned and challenged to determine their truthfulness. If we jumped off a bridge, stepped in front of a speeding car, or touched a hot stove element, would we be injured? The probability of serious injury is high, if not certain, but would we take the time to question and challenge this by doing those things? Hopefully not, but what about unprotected sex, drinking and driving, or substance abuse? Do we not understand the risk involved in them? Yes, we do, and yet some of us disregard them. We define Safety Net paradigms as, *"a perception that helps us to recognize danger and not make the same mistake twice."* Questioning and challenging these paradigms can lead to great personal harm and, at the same time, we may put others at risk of harm. How many people still have unprotected sex, with the danger of contracting AIDS or other sexually transmitted infections? How many people are killed or injured by drunk drivers every year, and yet people still do it? How many people begin or continue to smoke, excessively drink on a regular basis, use drugs, and ignore exercise, while knowing the risks involved? Safety net paradigms are in place to *catch our fall*, yet many of us continue to live with an indifferent or ignorant attitude toward them.

Most people we know will probably agree that making a change in one's life is a good thing, a healthy thing. Most of the time, it is as long as pro-social decisions motivate it. When someone chooses to change, it is a conscious decision, but when people change, he or she may not be aware of what they are doing. I am asking you to please be aware.

So far, I have hopefully handed you some insightful and thought-provoking material. With the information that I provided, I would like to look closer at how it works. Just like in grade 10 science class, the objective is to find the results of an experiment and why it reacts that way. We are about to look through a magnifying glass at how a belief is formed and spread. This experiment will be called the Paradigm Reactor. Please note that this experiment is highly secretive, and the result of this experiment may change your life forever.

WARNING: PROCEED WITH CAUTION!

EXPERIMENT

It is very late at night, and you are in the underground parking lot. You proceed to the elevator and press your floor selection. All of a sudden, you hear someone get on the elevator behind you, and your heart starts to beat very quickly.

Just like in all experiments, we must form a hypothesis, or a guess. Describe what you imagine this person looks like, and why you are scared. I will even assist in this experiment with some clues.

Clues

- Does the person have long, greasy hair?
- Does the person have tattoos?
- Does the person have scars?
- Is the person large or petite?
- Is the person clean shaven or do they have facial hair?
- Is the person black or white?

With all the clues that I gave, add some more of your own, and explain why you were scared. People, who were describing their greatest fears, most commonly used the clues given above.

The old saying is that you cannot judge a book by its cover. If you could describe a person from the clues provided, or from your own, the experiment was a success.

Step A

You see a person, place, or thing/situation.

Step B

You make a guess or assumption based on what you see.

Step C

You now act upon the information, in thought or action. A + B + C =Paradigm Reactor

Formal definition:

Information + model + theory + perception + assumption + frame of reference = Paradigm

This formula happens so fast that at times we do not even know what happened.

How many times have you looked at someone and assumed that they were something they were not? The Paradigm Reactor does not just happen in our perception of people; it happens in the way we see everything around us. For example, if we do not stay on our toes, we can be fooled even when we read.

PARIS IN THE

THE SPRING.

Read the above sentence out loud. Read each word out carefully, and don't skip any words. If you read it correctly, you will notice the word, *the*, in the sentence, which makes the sentence incorrect. If you did not see the two *THE*'s, it is because you formed a paradigm reactor, and you need to defuse it by examining and investigating the sentence. If you notice the way that both *THE*'s are positioned, you will see that they are not on the same line, and the sentence is short, so many people glance at the sentence and don't see both *THE'S.*

Once the Paradigm Reactor has been activated, the only way to avoid the fall out, which consists of conditioning, stereotyping, typecasting, and generalizations, is to DEACTIVATE THE PARADIGM.

DEACTIVATING THE PARADIGM

When a Bomb Squad is called to a dangerous situation, before defusing the bomb, they assess the situation and carefully examine the bomb. They know if they make one wrong move, the bomb may explode. Time is of the essence, and precision is required.

When DEACTIVATING A PARADIGM, the same principle applies to that of the Bomb Squad. To stop the explosion, we must first examine and study the source.

DEACTIVATING

A. We see a person, place or thing/situation.

B. We DON'T make a guess or assumption.

C. We scrutinize the situation and investigate all options.

D. We do not act upon anything unless we are 100% sure of the situation.

With the above information in mind, we want to think of a few Paradigm Reactor situations, as the Bomb Squad tries to deactivate the paradigm.

Here are a few paradigms that need to be deactivated:

- Blondes have more fun.
- Fat people are unattractive.
- Women are born to follow; men are born to lead.
- Asians are smarter than Caucasians.
- All blacks are criminals.

Notes

Notes

CHAPTER 8

What is R.E.A.L. Leadership?

Our society holds the concept of leadership and, subsequently, those who are leaders, in very high regard. These are individuals who, for one reason or another, have been elevated above their peers. These are individuals we look to in times of crisis, or whenever a decision is to be made and responsibility is to be taken. Therefore, we traditionally understand and recognize certain qualities leaders must possess, such as responsibility, effectiveness, accountability, stability, trustworthiness, decisiveness, guidance, and integrity. The perception of society's belief is that leadership is personified by those who *stand out from the crowd* by making decisions and choices, and being opportunistic on behalf of everyone else *in the crowd*. In effect, those who influence, guide, and direct the *crowd* are leaders. This scenario can undoubtedly have applied to some group situations, but what about personal leadership represented by our willingness to make decisions and be opportunistic for ourselves?

We nurture and educate our children to think for themselves and make their own decisions. It is a shame that, quite often, this means to *"be unique but not different."* All too often, a young person will form an idea utilizing an independent thought process, but then it is changed to suit the standards and expectations of society. The bottom line can read: You can *do what you want, but make sure you conform!*

I have been told that I am arrogant and conceited. Those that told me had come up with this conclusion without knowing me personally. I was told that I thought I was better than others because I always challenged the world around me. I would say, "Hey, I am not going to go with the flow on this one. I am not sure that what I am hearing or seeing is the truth, so I am going to examine and investigate to find out." This approach has and will continue to make people uncomfortable. Anytime people experience a challenge or change in what they believe to be the truth, it is painful. Hopefully, we experience this pain when we are affirmed.

What did we do to have people label us this way? I was a leader—nothing more, nothing less. We are demonstrating responsible, effective, and affirmed leadership, the second fruit to be harvested from having R.E.A.L. self-esteem. As we have already stated, our society is filled with well-established UNR.E.A.L. paradigms, of which we are often not aware. When it is questioned, those who believe and support UNR.E.A.L. paradigms feel as though they are being attacked; when, in fact, it is their belief system under scrutiny. This questioning will make people get out their 3-D glasses, so they can start denying, distorting, and defending, because they think they are living in the R.E.A.L. world; but, in fact, they are perceiving and believing in an UNR.E.A.L. world. It is the removal of those glasses that is painful. At no time did you tell those people, "Hey, what's wrong with you? You are wrong, and I am right, which makes me better than you, so you should listen to me and start following my lead." R.E.A.L. leadership does not work that way.

We know several people who have spent a great deal of their life preparing for a career that proved to be unfulfilling. High school and post-secondary decisions were always dependent on their need to fulfill that career. The resulting lifestyle soon became synonymous with them. They soon began to feel that their career, and everything they had done to attain it, was all they were recognized for. It soon consumed their identity.

Those people found that they had limited themselves to a certain degree by being focused on that career objective. Although that first career was significant to these people, it was no longer fulfilling. Every day, they went to work and felt like it was *punching the clock* and putting in their time. They soon realized, despite its importance in their life, they needed to feel more fulfilled. It was not a short time after this realization that they knew they had to take the first steps toward making a worthwhile and fulfilling change. For those individuals who made the change, it was not without backlash. Angry and confused criticism from friends and family would be a commonality. People would be quick to point out the sacrifice and dedication they put forth to attain that career.

It was very frustrating for me, at times, to listen to the comments and opinions of people I cared for and respected, but I knew how much I was sacrificing by not working at something that provided more satisfaction and happiness. I knew I had to find my truth somewhere else—so I did.

R.E.A.L. leadership is about making personal choices and decisions, based on the truth. It is about taking our reality at any given moment and changing it into our envisioned idealism. The decisions are reflected in the following four-step process:

1. Create a R.E.A.L. vision

The concept of "to lead" indicates there is some place to go. This place is a vision created by something we want to do. When we aspire to do something, when we imagine things we want to do or become, we create visions for ourselves. A vision is an aspiration, which can be anything from crossing the street to obtaining a PhD to flying to the moon or getting a part-time job. It does not matter what it consists of, as long as there is a destination in mind. We can, and will, create new visions all the time. When we do not have a vision, we will begin to live today, for today only, without the consciousness of a tomorrow or destination. When we lack vision, we become complacent and fail to lead ourselves. We will begin to live reactively by accepting a *Band-Aid*, or *quick-fix* measures. It will eventually make us susceptible to the vision of others. In doing so, we trade in our autonomy and become a follower of conformity. We will undermine our affirmation by taking responsibility and effectiveness out of our lives. Our efforts will lead us in the adoption of a *victim* stance, because there is no personal accountability or responsibility involved.

"Know where you are, and know where you are going" Create clarity, which is vital when it comes to a vision.

Close your eyes and visualize a green square, a red triangle, and an orange circle. You were able to see those shapes in your mind, even though your mind is clouded with other things.

2. Understand our choices

Once we have created a vision of what we want to do or become, the next step is to begin thinking about how we can fulfill. There will always be many choices available to help us make that vision reality. It is essential that we focus on considering all available choices that may assist us in this process. Even if they seem to be ridiculous or impractical at the start, we never know when any choice may present itself as plausible. Create a journal and record them somehow so that you can keep track of them for future reference. Make sure you are organized when proceeding with this step. It is these available choices that you are going to use as a basis for making your decisions.

3. Make self-confirming decisions

The list of choices available to us, all of which will help make our vision a reality, will consist of some that are *Band-Aids* or *quick fixes*, some that may be illegal or all wrong, and some that will confirm who we are. Our conscious willingness to make decisions that confirm and stay away from decisions that jeopardize our humanity and the humanity of others is what proves our self-esteem as being R.E.A.L. This means that our focus must be on doing what is right for us. Anything else means we will have become subservient to society's pressure by adhering to a standard or expectation in the form of an UNR.E.A.L. paradigm. If we want to make a R.E.A.L. decision, we must focus on a choice that confirms what we believe to be the truth.

4. Be accountable and responsible—Be a survivor

It is at this stage that you fulfill your self-esteem prophecy, and you will either adopt a *victim stance*, or you will become a survivor. As previously stated, some of our decisions can be of the quick fix, Band-Aid, illegal, or immoral variety. If this is the type of decision you make, you will set yourself up for the adoption of the *victim stance*, because you have not held yourself accountable. This type of decision will invalidate your humanity and, possibly, someone else's. It will fulfill the prophecy of low and UNR.E.A.L. self-esteem. When this happens, we will not hold ourselves accountable or responsible for our decisions and, until we do, we will continue to invalidate our self and others. We will not be able to raise our self to a level of R.E.A.L. self-esteem. Deciding and being able to hold ourselves accountable and responsible for the outcome, whether it is bad or good for us, will fulfill the R.E.A.L. self-esteem prophecy. Our willingness to intervene and affirm ourselves is what confirms and maintains our R.E.A.L. self-esteem. Not every decision will work out the way we expect, but if we are prepared to cope with the outcome, using personal accountability and responsibility, we would be able to move forward and make our vision reality.

To become R.E.A.L. leaders, we must move beyond what we believe traditional leadership to be. R.E.A.L. leadership is not about organizing others, making decisions on their behalf, or *taking them somewhere*, because this indicates a group of people as followers. We must be accountable for our lifestyle, our decisions, and ourselves. R.E.A.L. leadership is about personal leadership and survival.

It does not mean we want to undermine those who have demonstrated traditional leadership in the past. Those who show leadership are not only important on a personal level but also on a level that society may benefit from. Every time people incorporate a change into their lives, leadership is demonstrated.

At one time, air and space travel, cross-continent communication systems, personal computers, lasers, and the medical technology our world now has, was the stuff dreams were made of. Now they are real. People were responsible, effective, and affirmed enough to search for alternative solutions to different problems. We will not continue to move forward unless we question, and challenge established paradigms. This forward progress is not limited to science and technology; it is also applicable to what we believe about ourselves and others.

Being a responsible, effective, and affirmed personal leader eventually allows us to lead others. It can happen in one of two ways. When we take ownership and maximize our self-esteem by sifting our newfound paradigm, awareness will provoke the question and challenge every paradigm of our experience. We can do this indirectly or directly. Therefore, after our leadership has been established, it will be placed within the context of two other leadership systems, but before we can lead others, we must have the willingness to lead ourselves in a responsible, effective, and affirmed manner.

When we use our power of positive intervention to question a paradigm that is challenging our self-esteem—whether it is a racist or sexist joke, doing a line of cocaine, drinking a bottle of Jack Daniels to make ourselves feel better and get through the day, or to use violence when we feel we can no longer cope with or control a situation—we will become an indirect leader: a role model. If we think about the people or characters, we have used to copy our behavior, beliefs, clothing, language, employment, activities, etc., we should recognize them as being our role models. They are like living, breathing paradigms. Whether they are a politician, parent, friend, sibling, teacher, employer, sport/music/movie celebrity, or whatever—they have indirectly affected us. This is because we have never directly talked to them about those aspects of their personality or character that we base ours on. When we step forward and intervene to question and challenge something, we do not believe is the truth, we will be modeling a belief and behavior to those who experience it. Although we may not be directly telling them what to believe or why they should believe it, we are still creating an awareness that we are going to *go with the flow*. This awareness will have an incredible influence on people because we will make them recognize, and maybe even appreciate, and learn from it.

There will come the point when our awareness either motivates us to question our insight, or we will automatically provide it. This insight is our knowledge and understanding of the difference between what is R.E.A.L. and what is UNR.E.A.L. It will be at this point when our intervention shifts from being indirect to direct, because we will not just be questioning paradigms; we will be shifting them. By adopting this system of leadership, we will become a mentor to other people. We will begin to have a direct influence on people when we can look them square in the eye and tell them that what they are doing or saying doesn't reflect freedom, dignity, justice, or equality, because it is the truth. It will hold people accountable and responsible for their actions by making them take ownership of what they believe. Mentoring in this fashion will allow people an opportunity to become conscious survivors, instead of perpetuating an unconscious victim stance. It will also be an incredibly self-confirming experience.

I feel it is essential for us to remember that although role models and mentors will always be a significant part of our lives, we must not try to be exactly like them. We should not spend our efforts on becoming them because, if we do, we will jeopardize our willingness to lead ourselves. If we are not aware of the clear distinction between learning from them and being like them, we may impose limits on our willingness to create our vision, understand our choices, make self-confirming decisions, or to be responsible and accountable for our decisions. When our efforts are concentrated on becoming like someone else, our willingness to learn will be surpassed by the desire to emulate. It will result in a shift from R.E.A.L. leadership to following someone else's vision, understanding someone else's choices, and making decisions that affirm and confirm someone else. This process ultimately results in the absence of personal responsibility and accountability.

We find ourselves saying, "How did I get myself into this mess?" It is an important question, to be answered with clarity and understanding. I suggest keeping a journal, diary, or log of the experiences and decisions you have had and made. These events can be recorded on a daily or weekly basis, which is dependent on our organization and convenience. I realize it is essential for people to know and understand what they have done and where they have been.

As we read in chapter two, it is ineffective, irresponsible, and unaffirmed to deny, defend, or distort our experiences. They can be incredibly empowering to learn from, if we take ownership and incorporate the lesson in our life to help in the future. A great way to do this is to reflect on our lives on a daily or weekly basis.

When we make decisions, we consider all the choices available, but do we understand the potential result of each one? After we make our decisions, are we prepared to see them through to the end or change them if they do not work out? When we make decisions, do we respect our integrity and the integrity of others?

Hopefully, I have presented a clear depiction of what R.E.A.L. self-esteem is, and how we can develop it, because we want to begin discussing its importance and benefits. By affirming ourselves, and learning to understand paradigms, we will plant the seed of R.E.A.L. self-esteem. When we use our power of positive intervention to question and challenge paradigms, we will nurture our self-esteem. By maintaining responsible, effective, and affirmed self-esteem by fulfilling a R.E.A.L. self-esteem prophecy, we will eventually harvest the fruits that will grow.

The first fruit of R.E.A.L. self-esteem is the ability to resolve a conflict. According to its definition, R.E.A.L. self-esteem promotes responsible, effective, and affirmed communication. What does this mean? It means that when confronted with a possible conflict situation, we will be conscious of it, and we will be able to intervene in a positive manner. By doing this, we may be able to avoid conflict before it happens. Experiencing conflict first, and then having to deal with it reactively, can be extremely difficult depending on the severity of the problems and costs that result.

Ask yourself what the primary cause was of any conflict you have experienced in your lifetime? In your introduction to the book, I asked you to put aside everything you have learned and believed about our race, language, religion, socio-economic status, political platform, gender, or sexuality. I only wanted you to focus on your humanity. Hopefully, I have been able to do that because, at this point, we would want to make a conscious and effective focus on these learned beliefs. When we do this, what happens to our humanity and the humanity of others? Does it change if we consider our religion, race, language, gender, sexuality, socioeconomic status, or whether we are better or less than, or stronger or weaker than another? What we believe is that our humanity is better or less than, stronger or weaker than, or more wrong than someone else's. Is that the truth, or objective, scientific, and historical facts, or the distorted subjective perception of science and history that we so carelessly believe?

Although conflict can be identified in several different ways, when we use the following three definitions to determine what we believe to be true, we will understand what role political ideology, socioeconomic status, religion, race, ethnicity, gender, and sexuality has played in its evolution.

1. Actions involving different ideas, interests, beliefs, or people.

2. A mental struggle resulting from incompatible or opposing needs, drives, wishes, or internal/external demands.

3. A natural by-product of people having different needs, interests, ideas, goals, and realities.

It is the distortion of humanity that is the fundamental root of conflict in all three definitions. *"My way of doing things is better t than yours, because my way of thinking and my humanity is better than yours,"* dominates conventional thinking. When we think this way, we put up barriers that do not allow us to communicate in a responsible, effective, and affirmed manner. Thinking this way is like wearing 3D glasses. Sporting these glasses allows the movie to be just like real life, because of its three-dimensional appearance. No matter how real it may seem, it is still unreal. This is analogous to leading our lives according to UNR.E.A.L. paradigms, because they only allow us to see real life in 3D: they will cause us to Deny, Distort, and Defend what we say, do, hear, and experience. Raising our self-esteem to a R.E.A.L. level is like taking those 3D glasses off, so we do not have to rely on the distortion, defense, and denial of our perceptions.

"The truth will set you free."

Notes

Notes

Notes